Through the Eyes
of My Heart

Through the Eyes of My Heart

Witness, Poetry, and Prophesy

Dr. Shirley Anne Cox

Through the Eyes of My Heart: *Witness, Poetry, and Prophesy*

Published by Wheatmark™
610 East Delano Street, Suite 104
Tucson, Arizona 85705 U.S.A.
www.wheatmark.com

International Standard Book Number:
978-1-58736-829-5
Library of Congress Control Number:
2007924872

To those who teach me about Jesus:
Georgie, P.J., and Mac

Acknowledgements

Writing a book requires one pen and a hundred hearts. Many wonderful people have assisted me with this project.

I call my supporters the Order of Barnabas. We read about this man in the New Testament. His name means "Son of Encouragement." He traveled with the Apostle Paul on his first missionary journey. Each of us needs a Barnabas or two in our lives. Mine include Pastors Jim Maines, Georgie Rodiger, Bill Daum, Richard McAlear, Floyd Lawson, and Tricia Lowe. My sisters-in-Christ who have attended retreats with me at Camp El Camino Pines for the past twenty years have given time and energy to edit my book. These angels include Meaghan Ellis, Daryl Forman, Susan Yates, Roxanne Christ, Anne Mohr, Brenda Toepfer, Ellen Platts, and Cathy Alexander. My brother-in-Christ, Joe Girillo, has also been a great asset.

My Christian brothers and sisters at Bethany Lutheran and Trinity Lutheran in Pasadena, Grace Lutheran in Culver City, Episcopal Church of the Transfiguration in Arcadia, and the Spirit Alive Fellowship in Irwindale have surrounded me with love and non-failing support.

A very special thanks goes to Pati Bruce who did the cover art work. What a blessing it is to have her loyalty.

One important lesson I have learned from the Gospels is that I don't belong to myself. I belong to God and the community He has given me. To God be the glory!

Foreword

In *Through the Eyes of My Heart*, Dr. Shirley Cox has written a book about her love of Jesus. She uses both prose and poetry for this endeavor. It's a no-holds-barred book; her writing is simple and startlingly honest. On every page, the reader can see the joy in her relationship with God, and her struggles with her own human nature.

Many of her poems are reminiscent of the psalms in which the writer first converses with God or bemoans his own human circumstances, and then, at the end, remembers the glory of God and praises Him. It is easy to identify with her struggles. She has a very clear vision of her own unworthiness but this insight does not cause her to try and hide from God. She understands clearly that His love is unconditional and that His grace and mercy are abundant in their relationship.

In her poem, the *Foal of a Donkey*, she uses the Palm Sunday beast that Jesus rode into Jerusalem as a metaphor for herself. This work resonates with me as truth. The last lines conclude:

I still don't know why he chose me.
On my best days,
I'm stupid and ornery
and accomplish very little.
But I could tell that I was special to Him;
I could see myself reflected in His eyes
and I was beautiful
and that was enough.

In *Through the Eyes of My Heart*, Dr. Cox also writes with a keen sense of humor. She asked me earlier this year, on my birthday, what wisdom I had gleaned from my seventy-six years of life. I told her that most of us take life too seriously. She is obviously in agreement.

I have known Dr. Cox for twenty-five years. I have seen her grow from a milk-drinking to a meat-eating Christian. I am honored to be her Godmother. I expect that all who read this book will identify with it, be edified by it, and love God more dearly because of it.

The Reverend Dr. Georgiana Rodiger
Ordained minister and clinical psychologist

Introduction

This book is a collection of some of my poetry. Also included is an abbreviated form of my witness, and prophesy.

It is my prayer that a line, or verse contained in my writings will open the eyes of a nonbeliever or stir the heart of a believer who desires a more intimate relationship with God.

I have written a notation before each of the poems so that the reader has an idea of what prompted the specific subject or emotion.

My Witness

1982: I was a mess. My life didn't feel as good as my resume suggested it should. I lived in the "d" states...despair, depression, disappointment, defensiveness, dysfunction, and dammit-all. My mood was usually pissy. I apologize retrospectively to all who happened to be in my path.

I come from a family of determined people. We make things happen. We are homemade, handmade, and self-driven. Except for me. Even though I was educated, successful, and otherwise within the family guidelines, I was consumed with self-hatred. Quieting the force of my internal critics was my compelling mission. I tried several variations of eating disorders, and put myself on vacations with mega-doses of prescribed drugs.

I had a sense that I needed something other than me. Self-sufficiency is the rule in my family, so this was a rule breaker. I tried involvement. I love movements. I've done them all: civil rights, anti-war, feminism, vegetarian, Macrobiotic, astrology, even dancing naked at an ashram in the desert praising Bagwan. I tried throwing I Ching coins, reading tarot cards, and studying the lines of my palm.

Nothing brought relief from the self-loathing. Even exhausting myself running 10K races and backpacking along ridge routes didn't neutralize the agitation.

Then Brad Silverman entered the picture. He was a sixteen year old, full-of-life, Downs Syndrome student at Pasadena High School.

His parents had tried several special schools to help him. None worked out well. So Brad was sent to public school and mainstreamed. I was among his clueless teachers. We didn't know what to do with Brad so we just threw him in the pack with the other 30 students.

I taught a class which prepared students for the proficiency exam. Brad was with me for two years. One semester he was even in my first period 7:30 a.m. class. As I walked grumpily toward my classroom, he'd always be there waiting. "GOOD MORNING, Miss Cox! Isn't it a WONDERFUL DAY!" I'd mumble something like, "Uh, yeah, sure Brad" in response.

Brad was a hard-working student who never lost his concentration unless a pretty girl walked by. Then he, like almost all males his age, was seriously distracted. He loved to argue with me. He would insist that there was an easier way to do something, and I was keeping it a secret. He really was entertaining.

When Brad was finally ready, he took his proficiency exam and passed it with ease. He was exuberant! I told him that it was time to celebrate. He should go home and tell his parents that they were taking us out to dinner. Again, massive enthusiasm on his part. We set a date and his parents took us to a fancy establishment for the finest prime rib available. It was indeed festive.

The power was out in Pasadena that evening; we ended our dinner by candlelight. When we separated in the parking lot, Brad hugged me. I felt a jolt of electricity go through my whole body as if Brad had captured what the city had lost. I was euphoric, and stayed that way for days. I had no idea what was happening to me but I suspected it had something to do with God. I don't know why I knew that because I surely didn't have any knowledge or experience of God. I was unchurched. My family just didn't do God.

I did know enough to look for a church. I was pretty sure God lived there. I wanted a church where the people were intelligent, concerned about the conditions of the world, and not too demonstrative. I found a Unitarian Church that fit my requirements.

I went to a service and sat quietly observing. My attention span is no longer than about 30 seconds. I found myself reading ahead in the bulletin. The phrase "when the perfect comes, the imperfect shall pass away" was written in the margin of the second page. I had no clue what it meant, but I was blown away by its intensity. The rest of the service was a blur; I was floating to higher places.

For two weeks, I walked three feet off the ground. I was mellower than I had ever been. Finally, I asked my friend Georgie Rodiger what she thought was happening. I think she knew I wasn't ready for a hell-and-brimstone witness, so she just explained that my little Jewish friend Brad was pure, and when he hugged me, I picked up his joyful energy field.

Georgie suggested that I visit her friend Edith Drury and ask if she could help me with my eating disorders. Surprisingly, I called. I wasn't too fond of strangers and was very self-conscious about the ways I was coping with life. I not only called; I scheduled a time to see her and actually showed up. We chatted a bit, and she asked if she could pray for me. I was into new mystical experiences, so I said, "sure." She laid hands on me and began to pray a lovely prayer of healing. I felt waves of electricity rolling through my body. She began speaking in a way I thought was very poetic… "His burden is easy and His yoke is light." I was at peace; the internal critic was finally silenced. I became absolutely chatty, asking Edith about the electricity and her poetry. Edith, who would rather grunt than speak, was very patient with me. She asked me to return the following week for a Bible study.

This was too good a feeling to lose, so I returned the next week.

She showed me a Bible, explaining that it was basically in two parts separated by a few hundred years. The first part was the Old Testament and the second part, the New Testament. She explained the difference between books, chapters, and verses. The first books of the New Testament, she told me, were the gospels. They told about the life of Jesus. She recommended I read Luke in a beginner's Bible. Sure, why not, I thought.

I read through Luke and understood almost nothing. It didn't matter. It was the most exciting stuff I had ever encountered. I called Edith and she told me to read the other gospels, and to stay away from the very last book in the Bible. I showed up at Bible study the next week; Edith was notorious for collecting strays. There was an assortment of marginal people; I fit right in. The thought question she started with was "Can the blind lead the blind?" By that time, I was so excited about Jesus, that I said, "I suppose so, if Jesus wanted it to happen." I think I ruined her lesson plan.

I met again with Edith the following week after reading through the gospels three or four more times. I had also picked up Agnes Sanford's books from Georgie, and some C. S. Lewis. I even read Oswald Chambers with absolutely no understanding. That didn't seem to matter. Everything I read excited me more. I couldn't get enough. Edith asked me if I were a Christian. I answered, "I don't think so; I haven't applied anywhere."

She asked me if I thought Jesus Christ was the Son of God who had risen from the dead and if I wanted him as my Lord. No brainer. "Of course," I said. She told me she was leaving for her summer home in Maine in two weeks, and wanted me to get baptized before she left.

This should be easy, I thought. I went to a huge church on Colorado Boulevard the next Sunday. There were several ministers. I planned to just ask one to baptize me after the service. During the service, the communion elements were passed down the pews. I knew I couldn't yet participate, but for the life of me I couldn't understand why the people were so gloomy. Why weren't they dancing on the pews?

After church, I went outside where people mingled and looked for a minister. There were four of them, all talking to each other. I waited for about ten minutes and then left. This baptism stuff wasn't as simple as it had been in John's time.

I was hang dog all afternoon. Another friend, Kay Templeton, had been helping me with all the words I didn't understand (which was most of them), e.g., salvation, redemption, atonement, ascension, justification, purification, resurrection, grace, mercy, disciple, apostle, and many, many others. Kay asked me if I wanted to go to a concert at her church. I didn't have any other plans except to get more depressed so I took her up on her offer.

The choir was so small at Kay's little Lutheran Church that members of a local Methodist congregation were invited to join them.

The pastor, a rather handsome man with a mop of wavy hair and a corduroy jacket with elbow patches, introduced the performance.

The first thing I noticed was that the church shook when anybody walked up the aisle. Rather shoddy construction, I thought.

The performance started and I began to cry. I never stopped. The choir started with old spirituals, and after intermission, they sang the *Messiah*. I had never heard any of it before. I was stunned by its impact. I left the church and cried for hours.

I called the church the next morning and asked to speak to the reverend person. The secretary told me his name was Pastor Jim Maines, and she put me through to him. When I heard the name *Maines*, I knew that God was sending me to him because Edith told me to get baptized before she left for *Maine*. I introduced myself to Pastor Maines and told him that he was supposed to baptize me.

Perpaps he thought my demand a little strange, but he didn't miss a beat. He simply asked me to drop by his office.

When I got to his office and repeated my sure knowledge that he was to baptize me, he asked for a little more of my story. Because I was so new to religion, I had no idea my story was beyond the pale of the ordinary. My only Christian contacts were Georgie, Edith, and Kaye; C.S. Lewis, Agnes Stanford, and Oswald Chambers; I didn't know that they were all part of a fringe group of deeply committed Christians who were called charismatics. Pastor Maines listened without saying much. Then he began asking very pointed questions: "What have you read that Agnes wrote...how do you understand the healing that you received from Edith's prayer...how do you know that I am the one who should baptize you...what happens when you read the Bible...have you had any visions...do you understand the commitment you are making?"

And then Pastor Maines broke the news to me. My experiences were not the same as those of most

Christians. He confided that he too believed as I did, but the congregation didn't know. They would not take kindly to the information. Believers like us were thought to be over-the-top, and more than a little unstable. Then he handed me some tapes by John Wimber and told me he would baptize me Sunday.

During the few days between the talk with Pastor Maines and my baptism, I was tormented. The internal introjects who were usually critical became terrifying. I had to call Kay for phone prayers each night in order to sleep. Each day after teaching, I would sit in Georgie's library and study the pictures in the book, *He Was One of Us*, until it was time to go home to bed.

I asked Kay and Georgie to be my Godmothers. Leah, another friend who was in New York, was my Godmother in abstentia.

When we got to the church, I was so antsy that I had trouble not running to the nearest exit. Georgie must have sensed my agitation because she held firmly to the back of my belt during the actual baptism.

A few days later, Pastor Maines, who by then was "P.J.", asked me to stop by after school each day to help him pray for people. Thinking this was a part of the Christian experience, I didn't hesitate. Two years later I learned that there were Christians who didn't believe Jesus was alive and active. He was just historic and the spiritual gifts were only for the early church. I found it confusing. Why would anybody want to just study Jesus when they could experience Him in the present?

I read further into the New Testament. Now I devoured the books which I called the Armenian books because they ended in "ian"...Galatians, Corinthians, Ephesians, Colossians. I identified heavily with St. Paul. Here was a man after my own heart... "why is it that I do what I would not do..." I could feel his dual nature which seemed much like my own. I found kinship with Paul. I also read about the Gifts of the Spirit, though I didn't yet quite grasp the concept of a triune God. I thought these gifts were wonderful. I wanted several of them. I even thought I read about the gift of hostility, which was right up my alley. Upon closer inspection, it was the gift of hospitality. Pass on that one. But I did look through the "menu" and ask God for almost all the others. Again, it was years later before I realized that even deeply committed Christians politely asked only for one or two gifts.

P.J. took me down to the Vineyard where John Wimber was speaking. There were some other people in my church with us. They were on a looky-lou field trip rather than a quest, as P.J. and I were.

Wimber was teaching the gift of discernment to the hundreds in attendance. He asked the congregation to speak what they were hearing from God in terms of healings available that evening. Wimber asked for participation only from people who had never shared such words before. There were many words, even some with specific numbers of sufferers. It was a terrific evening's entertainment. Finally, when the front of the church was packed with those for whom the words were intended, Wimber said, "I hope there's nobody out there trying to hide some-thing, because God is here in strength tonight."

I was trying to hide something. I breathed a sigh of relief when the word gifts came to a close. Now, we'd watch the praying. Suddenly, Wimber said, "Oh, hold on for a moment. God just told me we missed somebody whose eating disorder has re-turned with a vengeance." I was busted. Oh, no. I thought I'd just ignore him. But it were as if a huge magnet was pulling me out of my seat and up to the front. I was tripping over people from my church… "excuse me, excuse me…excuse me." I got up front where the prayer teams were already at work. A young girl approached me. She was so young I was tempted to ask her curfew time. She put a hand out toward me, and down I went, BAM! After getting over the initial shock and failing in my attempts to get up, I relaxed into the inevitable. The air in the room became wonderfully textured. I could almost feel it. The peace was so pervasive, I wanted to stay there forever. I began to realize that God was kindly giving me a foretaste of Heaven. The girl was talking to me while I was down, basking in bliss. "God says you don't have to do it anymore. He'll give you the power you need." The next thing I knew I was be-ing grabbed by the kind folks from my church who thought I had fainted. So much for a slice of Heaven! The girl asked me, as I was being taken away, the na-ture of the problem for which she had just prayed. She didn't even know! Her faith in God's sufficiency was awesome.

1982-2006: You'll have to read my book, which

I have not yet written, to get this story. It's like Jesus' story between lost at the temple and dunked in the River Jordan by John...years of mystery.

2006: When I look at my salvation history, I am still amused that God chose a light-filled Jewish boy to witness to me. Then, He put me in a church with the only charismatic Lutheran pastor in miles. P.J. is also Jewish by birth but Christian by call.

Twenty four years later, I'm still one of the fringe Christians. God uses me and even better, he adores me. My passion waxes and wanes, but I never lose sight of what's absolute. God's sacrifice, God's love, God's faithfulness, God's mercy and grace...these are Absolute.

I have no questions about my own worthiness. I tried life without God. I failed. I'm not a squeaky-clean sort of Christian. I'm marginally charitable, infrequently nice, and usually absorbed with myself.

I've often thought it was to my advantage to come late into the Kingdom. I could be one of the laborers who did only a couple hours work, and still received full wages! Even better, I had no confusion about who picked whom. I think cradle Christians sometimes think they found God. There's no doubt in my mind. God found me, and I wasn't much. Now he uses me; I'm still not much. However, I always know that the river runs from Him to me. Our relationship is real. I am the other end of the pious continuum from most of the people I know. My identity is with Mary Magdalene and the Disciple Paul. I was forgiven much; I love fiercely in response.

Selected Poetry

This poem was written specifically for Dr. Georgiana Rodiger, my Godmother, but it also seems appropriate for all my Christian friends.

A Lenten Blessing for my Godmother

March 5, 2003

May you find the sustaining love from Jesus
    that even friends cannot give.
May you hear His wisdom
    in the quiet of the night;
    a wisdom that befuddles the world.
May you see through His eyes,
    and through His tears.
May you share His suffering,
    not from His pain,
    but for the lostness of His children.
May you be absorbed by His journey,
    may it become your pressing reality.
May you welcome the darkness,
    as He did.
May you be strengthened for the battle
    with the sure knowledge
    that He is with you
    always.

A Lenten reflection.

Rebellion

February, 2001

Heavenly Father,
Beloved Son,
giver of life,
forgive me for my insistence
on my right to sin;
my persistence in
wrong doing,
wrong thinking,
wrong heartedness.

If I could rid myself
of my constant transgressions,
I'm not sure I would,
so familiar are they,
so painfully comfortable,
so wonderfully mine.

Create in me
a new heart
that never met the old one,
new vision,

new capacity to love
in ways other than
what has always been.

I feed my flame
of rebellion,
willfully, spitefully,
I claim a right to myself,
as I profess you,
and I am both ashamed of myself
and delighted with myself.

Why am I so distinctly
of two minds?
proud of my darkness,
enamored of your light in me.
And why is the darkness so solid
and the light so fragile?

Will I ever be more like you
than unlike you?
Will I ever find
my darkness
so distasteful
that I will be willing
to be stripped of it,
and will you still be there
to do it?

You are the fisherman;
how much line
will you give me?
I grow weary of the struggle.

Will you accept
my surrender
if most of the internal army
refuses
to disengage from the battle for self?
If only one or two
want to be on your side?

My foolishness
will lead me to death;
I play with sharp edges
and hampered vision.

Help me, Lord,
I'm on a path of chaos
and I can't
get myself to stop
or even care.

Holy week is a difficult week for me as it is for most Christians. In this poem I encounter the pain of my sin.

Monday

Holy Week, 2001

Dear Jesus,

You climbed the hill for me,
you accepted the pain for me,
you were mocked for me,
you died for me,
you forgave me.

My tears stream
as my spirit wrestles with shame,
and my heart with grief
because your light
illumes my darkness
and I feel so unclean.

Let me walk with you this year,
If I can,
my steps so small
compared to yours
and my courage so little

compared to yours.

Because you died for me,
I do not want to be in the world
in a way that continues
to cause you pain
because that would be the only pain
I couldn't endure.

I did a lot of writing during Lent, 2002. This silly story
is one of my favorites because it fits so well.

Lamb

March, 2002

One lamb,
a bit stupid,
a bit curious,
a bit ornery,
mostly oblivious…
would wander to the edge
of the fold
and wish her world
were bigger.

So the Shepherd
opened the gate
and she trotted off,
mostly oblivious…
(Unbeknown to her,
He stayed with her.)

With joy
she explored,
tasted,

sniffed,
rubbed against,
watched,
mostly oblivious…

She was happy,
warm,
contented,
eager.

But night came
with its sounds
and chill,
its emptiness,
loneliness,
jumbled memories
and the lamb was afraid.

She looked for a
place to hide,
another lamb
to cuddle,
a voice to soothe,
a place of safety,
now sharply aware,
still stupid,
but no longer oblivious.

She turned,
saw the Shepherd,
leapt into
His outstretched arms.

I had fun writing this one. I seem to write easily from the position of an ass.

The Foal of a Donkey

Palm Sunday, 2006

I saw the two men in rags approach.
They untied me.
They said the man with the bright eyes
needed me.
I didn't understand why.
I'm the foal of a donkey,
    not easy to look at
    not too bright
    don't do much
but he chose me anyway,
wanted to ride me,
I'd never carried anyone before.

He was gentle,
I knew what He needed though He didn't
speak.
He was a light burden
but I could feel His heavy heart.
I'm an outcast;
I knew He was too.

We rode into Jerusalem.
The people were packed together,
    shouting.
      throwing things in front of me.
I would have been frightened
    and run away
except He needed me
and was with me
and I was at peace.

I still don't know why he chose me.
On my best days,
    I'm stupid and ornery
    and accomplish very little.
But I could tell that I was special to Him;
I could see myself reflected in His eyes,
and I was beautiful
and that was enough.

I wrote this during an Easter Eve service at the Episcopal Church of the Transfiguration in Arcadia.

Easter Eve, Church

March 31, 2002

Splendor,
    magnificence
    abounding love,
    have all come
    to this moment.

The darkness
    watches
    disdainfully,
    looking to devour
    the weak.

Strengthen me,
O Beloved Savior
    so that I might
    survive
    the attacks
    of the evil around me,
    the evil within me.

Weary,
    I am unable to fight alone.
Where have we gone?
Why have you let me stray?

When will you
    capture me again?
Bring me back into
    your arms,
    sanctuary from myself.
I will wait,
    believing desperately
    that what I sever,
    you will heal.

The cross
    brings me agony,
    makes me face
    my self-love
    with contempt.

Yet I cannot
    escape the encompassing
    selfishness
    any more than
    I can flee
    my shadow.

Wrestle with me,
    Lord,
and be victorious.

I am very grateful to my Godmother, Georgie Rodiger, for saving my life and teaching me about God (again saving my life). I have written a lot of appreciation and thank you poetry to her.

Thoughts for my Godmother

Easter, 2003

She thinks of herself
    as "friend of God"…
I think of her as
    child of Jesus,
    set apart,
    vaguely connected here,
but not with the same passion
that links her to Jesus.

She thinks of herself
    as a clay pot
    yielded to the Potter…
I think of her as
    His Light,
    formless,
    dynamic,
    pervasive,
moving at His discretion.

She thinks of herself
    as His hands, His feet,
    His ears, His eyes...
I think of her
    only
    as His heart,
carrying His wounds,
His love,
His joy,
His compassion,
His hope.

She thinks of herself
    as His tool...
I think of her as
    His open arms,
offering herself
    endlessly,
relying on Him
    to sustain her.

She thinks of herself
    as a mirror...
I think of her
    as a prism,
showing forth
His love in all
its manifestations
to the spiritually
impoverished.

She thinks of herself
    as a plodder,
    working for her Lord
    with great determination...
I think of her
    as a dancer,
    light as love,
    gracefully offering
    a bedazzling
    holy beauty.

I'm afraid I'm clueless about the circumstances of this
poem.

At the Wedding

February, 2001

It was God's moment,
the view was His,
the people were His,
the blessings were His.

Time was suspended
as were the boundaries
among the people.
The scene had only unity.

The glimpse was of
eternity and infinity,
perfect,
divine,
a blending of the disjointed
with one brush stroke,
an instant of all time
and all things.

Transcendent,
confusing to consider,
nonsensical to verbalize.

We are His.
His is everything,
always,
encapsulated
in each second of non-time
in every place,
in every person,
without distinction.
He struck me dumb,
delighted,
terrified,
humbled
that He should see me.

Awesome Love
touched me,
briefly, completely,
and then backed away,
knowing I could
tolerate no more.

I wrote this at a Lutheran Retreat at a Catholic Retreat
Center in the San Fernando Valley. I was walking the
stations of the cross, feeling overwhelmed at the story
they tell.

At the Stations of the Cross

February 23, 2000

First station,
standing uneasily
confessing to you
my indifference,
my lack of gratitude,
my hard-heartedness.

Moving,
station to station,
losing words,
losing awareness,
weak-kneed,
now only sensation,
alone with you.

How ashamed
I suddenly become
as I see the station

with the women
surrounding your body
and feel their pain;
inconceivable loss.

I reach out to them
offering the sting
of my tears.
Let me weep with you,
broken sisters,
during this moment
of infinity,
time stopped,
as your souls tear,
touching the lifeless body
of the Beloved.

Let me comfort you
as you wait
for that which you know not;
hope sustaining you
as life cannot.

Include me in your despair,
teach me your agony
that I may better know Him,
and let me wait with you
until the Light returns.

Again, I'm unsure of my situation when writing this poem. I seem to spend a lot of energy sorting out my ideas of God.

Gentle God

April, 2003

I refuse to enter
    into a place of despair
Where my fragile spirit
    will collapse.

I cannot believe
    that the hand with
    which you hold me
    would also crush me,
    although I know that it could.

If I accept you as rageful,
    vindictive, impatient,
I will need to flee,
for then you will be too much
    like me.

Another intimate moment. I don't remember the
circumstances.

Surrounded by God

December, 1999

Surrounded by God,
    no words,
    no thoughts,
    no images,
    just palatable presence.

I savor the sensation;
God the cloud,
    containing me,
    defining me,
    adoring me.

I surrender
    to the loveliness
    of the moment.
Stay, Lord,
This is the marital bed,
    pure love,
    heady stuff,

strength in softness,
strength in pervasiveness.

Stay, Lord.

But, alas,
    the contact breaks.
I cannot sustain it.
No capacity for
    anything
    so wonderful,
    so absolute.

Somday, I too
shall be Light,
like You,
with You.

Until then,
I wait,
a taste, sufficient.

When I wrote this, I was thinking gratefully about the (God)mother who has been given to me.

(God)mother's Day

May, 2004

Who is my mother?
she who does the will of the Father.
Who is my mother?
she who loves as does the Son.
Who is my mother?
she who contains the Spirit.

Heavenly dyads
created to sustain us
until we shed these earthly minds
with their chaotic cadences
and unending fickleness.

God's richest earthly blessing,
our companions on the journey
who alter their strides
for a season
so that we may walk next to them,
learn a new pace,

acquire another set of eyes,
a more peaceful perspective.

Thank you, Mother from God,
for your obedience,
steadfastness,
selflessness,
capacity to contain,
unwavering commitment to Him.

He is the Alpha and Omega,
you, the letters in between.

This is a good bye to a friend. God has given me
numerous, loving friends. Inevitably, the season with a
friend is shorter than I'd like.

My Friend Leaves

November, 2001

Thank you, Lord
for companions on the journey
whose wounds
reflect our own,
whose hearts
are also fragile,
whose perseverance
gives us strength,
whose tears of love
water our souls.

Given our nature, Lord,
we would hold tightly
to these friends
forever.
But such is your nature
and your love,
that you wrest them from
our tenacious grasp,

and ask us to trust you,
your graciousness,
your enduring mercy,
your eternal steadfastness.

Lord, with heavy heart,
I thank you for my friend,
who walked with me
a minute in my life of eternity,
reminding me of you,
and giving me a taste of
love as you have created it to be.

This poem was written in appreciation of the women in my Friday morning prayer group at Blair High School. I was about to retire. These women were great blessings to me.

Blair High School Prayer Group

June, 2003

Dear Sisters in Christ,

He has given you to me
    as companions on my journey
    and now you are part of my salvation
        history
    as I am part of yours.

You have sustained me,
    given me strength,
    increased my courage.

You live now in my heart
    which is richer because of you,
    His gift of mercy.

We finish our weekly prayers today
    but the love we share
    will be eternally
    embedded in my heart.

If no other evidence of God existed
    than you,
      it would be sufficient.

I don't even remember the identity of the friend in
trouble, but I sense that I certainly was irked at God.

A Friend in Trouble

January, 2002

God,
Why are you putting her through this?
    Sliding into darkness,
        terror, despair, rage,
        a widening abyss.

Touching to the depths
    of her own soul,
        and finding things she
        cannot bear.

She sways,
    life in one hand,
    death in the other,
        waiting for a wind of hope,
        or a word of permission.

You have known her
    since the beginning of time,
    knit her together in her

mother's womb,
have counted every hair.

You have created her
for your pleasure,
a sweet fragrance of love.

You have set her lines in pleasant places.
Can there be any way for her to grasp
a love which seems to abandon,
a vigilance that lets evil slide by?

Oh, Lord,
she does not understand;
release her from the need to;
she is wearied by the battle,
be a shield for her;
she surrenders to your
holy hands,
mold her gently;
increase her faith,
that she may praise you
in her brokenness.

Draw her gently to your heart
and mend hers,
restore her peace;
let the light in her,
once again,
burst forth in radiance.

Amen

This was a Christmas Eve poem which I wrote as I looked at the figures in the small Nativity at the front of the church.

Baby Boy

Christmas, 2004

Baby boy
on your mother's breast
already an outcast,
unmoving,
except for the radiance
of your eyes,
searching the hearts
of those around you.
Let me be there, too,
bowing,
awed and confused by your
tiny, helpless perfection.
Your existence lays bare the shame
of my humanness;
my darkness drives me
to despair.
I see Mary the Innocent
and Joseph the Courageous

cleansed by their Obedience.
Of these qualities, I have none.
Is there room for me?

I wrote this at a retreat in Arizona with the theme of "Hope." I'm ashamed to admit that I still struggle with surrender and often demand the right to control my own life.

Hope

November, 2005

Hope invites me to ask her in.
I resist.
I tell her,
> "if I invite you in,
> you'll steal my resolve
> and leave me defenseless."
She says,
> "if you don't let me in,
> you'll serve an empty god
> and your heart will die."
I answer,
> "can I not substitute
> unceasing effort for hope?"
"No" she responds,
> "you must substitute
> unceasing hope for effort."
I ask,
> "how do I get from

here to there?"
She says,
"believe that God
can sew hope in your heart
and breathe new life into you;
offer yourself to Him,
not your idea of yourself,
rather, His idea of you."
I reply,
"I offer me in Him to Him in me?"
She nods,
"exactly."

This was a prayer I wrote at a silent retreat at the
Episcopal Church of the Transfiguration.

Silent Retreat

January, 2002

Lord,
Let me esteem others
    and not myself.
Let me unfold according
    to your vision.
Let me not view myself
    as above others
    in my own sight
    or in yours.
Let me hope only
    for closeness to you.
Let me dread only
    separation from you.
Let me be awed by
    our intimacy,
    your majesty,
    your willingness to bear
        pain for me.
Let me learn to
    open my ears

and not my mouth.
Let me learn to walk gently
    amidst the grandeur
    of your creation.
Let me battle only against
    my sin,
        sin habitual,
        sin defensive,
        sin aggressive,
        sin of separation.
Let me surrender
    my unwillingness
        to surrender.
Let my eyes be vigilant
    only to discover you
    in every person,
    and not seek
    my own reflection.
Let me be
    willing to walk,
    willing to stop,
    willing to turn.
Let my passions endlessly
    seek you.
Let my heart know
    the rhythm of yours.
Lord, Jesus Christ,
    I offer all that I am,
    please receive that
    and gently claim
    the I am that I don't know.

Amen

I was at the Catholic Charismatic Renewal when I wrote this reflection on the shame of my darkness.

Steubenville

June, 2005

You came quietly
last night
in a whisper unheard,
except by me,
touched my brokenness,
my rage and terror,
absorbed my darkness,
again,
and left your peace.

How sweet is your love,
how generously given,
signature of your
eternal mercy.

Will you teach me,
Keeper of my Heart,
to look past the absurdity
of my own life design
and trust yours?

Can you persuade me,
Eternally present Lord,
to abandon my perceived safety
and embrace your unknown?

How often you have forgiven
my smallness,
my slowness,
my sameness.
How patiently you wait,
forgiving my digressions,
my transgressions.

I need most that
which I fear most.
I cannot transverse the chasm.
Will you answer
even when I cannot ask?

Lord of all that I am or will be,
let your love carry me;
let your sufficiency be my joy.

I remember this women's retreat clearly. I was in a place of great despair which probably resulted in the desperate honesty I sense in this poem.

Women's Retreat

October, 1999

Jesus,
most beloved, sought-after,
Lamb of the Father,
Lamb of my heart.

In your eyes
I see my tears.
My soul agonizes,
too small
to absorb
the intensity of your love.

I cannot draw closer,
alternately raging and terrified,
ashamed of my darkness,
afraid of your light.

But you are my constant,
yours is the siren song,

haunting.
I cannot turn away.

Reach for me, O Lord,
because I cannot come closer.

Hold onto me, O Lord,
because I cannot sustain
my grasp of you.

Believe in me, O Lord,
because I am so congested
with self-distain
that I cannot persevere.

Free me, O Lord,
to become not me
because I cannot balance
both of us.

Feed me, O Lord,
because nothing else fills.

Let me rejoice in you,
the loveliness of your touch,
the softness of your kiss,
the satisfaction of your embrace.

Jesus, my Lord, beloved,
designer of all my yearnings,
possess me,

endlessly.
Be not deterred
by me.

A moment of clarity with my God and my friends at a women's retreat.

El Camino Pines

May, 2002

He intends that
    we live fully;
beyond what
    we can imagine;
riches undefinable.

He spreads a table before us
    here, now,
a table laden with
    joy
and constant miracles for those
    not afraid to see
    the things that blind the world.

Our only response is
    awe,
    tears of wondrous bewilderment;
    hunger for more of Him,
    a heart pained by love too large,
    an overwhelming passion

to adore Him
always,
unceasingly.

The world is
an irritant,
demanding time and energy from
our preferred communion
with Him.
For He is our day and night,
unfathomable treasure,
unending source of awakenings;
our beloved, our betrothed,
our Jesus.

This poem is typical middle-of-the-night doubts put in perspective.

Nighttime

December 12, 2001

Inert,
but partially alert,
trying to give form
to the chaotic
disjointed pieces
demanding
center stage
in my mind.

Am I failing,
Lord,
as your chosen,
set aside,
to accomplish
something
imaginable only
to a totally
surrendered heart?

Edge of euphoria,
delightful tension,
senses on full alert.

Waiting for you;
how delightful we will be.
For now,
sadness, fear, anger,
disappointment, emptiness,
confusion.
But only for now.

This poem was written at the Episcopal Church of St. George in La Canada. It is an attempt to explain the vision I received the previous night while my friend Mary Lou so beautifully sang the Lord's Prayer.

Vision from the Lord's Prayer

January, 2007

Surrounded by a silence of your own,
    protecting you from the cutting jeers,
you proceed slowly to Calvary
    little more to be said,
    one thing left to do.

Your Mother's pain drives her to her knees;
the only relief ,
    her face uplifted to the
    healing warmth of the Father's love.

You humbly submit to death by hatred,
    forgiving your debtors,
    then and now,
    absorbing all sin.
Your spirit abandons your battered body,
    ripped off the cross,
    an empty vessel,

an emblem of sin destroying,
sin destroyed.

How painful to wait in darkness
for your promised return,
no longer able to fend off
    doubt and self hatred.

Then suddenly,
    in the brutal hours of the longest night
the Father's love breaks through,
    in the beatuty of
    the magnificent sunrise,
causing the shadow of the cross
to lengthen far enough
    to touch hearts fovever.

We try and understand other people. We always fall
short. The more God has captured them, the less we can
know them. This is my attempt to characterize a saint.

To Georgie

Maundy Thursday, 2006

You've been in His heart
    since the beginning of time.
He delighted in creating you,
    and you delight in Him.
You are His beloved daughter.

He feels each bruise
    the world gives you,
and notices your courage.
    and unwavering focus
    on His mercy,
    on His grace,
    and is pleased.
You are His beloved daughter.

He hears you calling to Him
    with unceasing praise.
"I love you Lord, and I lift my
    voice to worship you,

oh my soul rejoice."
He dances to your music,
    His heart overflowing with joy.
You are His beloved daughter.

He watches you witness,
    cheerfully,
    authentically,
    passionately,
He is honored by your faithfulness.
You are His beloved daughter.

He cheers you on,
as does all of the Heavenly Host
    as you feed his sheep,
    and bring the lost ones
    into the fold.
He is proud.
You are His beloved daughter.

He's given you a child's eyes,
    each new day a new unfolding,
    another adventure,
    a joyful memory.
He shows you that
    Creation is your playground.
Trusting Him, you follow your path,
    because He encourages you.
You are His beloved daughter.

He drops the troubled ones
    on your doorsteps,
assured of your selflessness.
You take them in
    and offer a place of safety
    as He does.
Your heart knows
    what your heart knows
    because He has instructed it.
You wash the feet of those He sends.
You are His beloved daughter.

He's given you a community
    of believers
    who love you,
    who learn from you,
    who feed you,
    who lift you in prayer,
    who walk beside you.
You are His beloved daughter.

His journey for you is
    everlasting,
    everloving.
Each day's peace promises another.
From the beginning of time
throughout Eternity,
    He is with you.
You are His beloved daughter.

I wrote this prayer on my third pilgrimage to the Holy Land.

Prayer Reflection on the Holy Land

April, 2005

Lord,
I walked where you walked,
I cried where you cried,
I saw the beauty
of the land
seeded by your blood,
seeded by your love.
Teach me,
Lord of my heart,
to put down roots
in your broken body
so that I can grow
as a reflection of You;
obedient,
humble,
open,
needful of nothing
but

the vision of seeing You
face-to-face,
love dancing from your eyes,
my home eternal.

Amen

I'm not sure what this is. I think it is about God's grace.
I wrote it on a pilgrimage to Italy.

To God

Italy, 2000

Quietly,
mercy unfolds,
cleanses,
enters fully,
claims,
silently possesses,
heals,
overflows,
is offered back to God,
a sacrifice of praise,
of love purified.

I was on a pilgrimage to Russia, awed and inspired by
the icons I saw. I had a rather shocking sense of my
absurdity.

Russia

August, 2005

Forgive me, Lord
for making you in my image,
a toy for amusement,
a pocket-sized friend,
a non-critical father
    who smiles at me.

For you are not my creation,
    snuggly, predictable.
I am yours.
You have made me,
my lips acknowledge you,
while my heart,
    worships my flaws,
    ignoring the nobility of
    your abiding excellence.

I profess my piety in public
instead of secretly seeking you

in trembling and awe.
I have little interest
    in Kingdom living
    beyond that which
    amuses or edifies me.

My faith is self-serving,
    erratic, shallow, irreverent,
    and nonsensical.
Forgive me, Jesus,
You are the Christ.
I have ignored you,
sold you short,
diminished you,
witnessing only to the
darkness in me.

Heal me, Lord.
my unworthiness is vast,
my arrogance,
crushes me with shame.

I dance in a circle, alone.
I despise my fearfulness.

I no longer want
    to offend you.
Yet, I do not believe
    I can yield,
terrified to sell everything
    and follow You.

Forgive me.
Change my heart.
Make sufficient the
    small amount of permission
    I can give to make me yours,
or destroy me.
I will not be a false witness.
I cannot continue to live for me
    and for you.
The battle is too wearying.

My love poems to Jesus are my favorites. This one was written on a Pilgrimage to Italy during the Year of Jubilation.

A Love Song

Italy, 2000

How lovely I am
    when you
    are present.
Your love sneaks up
    and consumes me.
I am softened by it
    and absorbed into
    a time of needlessness;
everything blocked
    but the textures
    of the moment.
Distinctiveness
    blurs into a
    boundaryless totality.

I understand
    that love is truth
    when you are with me;
unexpectedly,

unsummoned,
    you appear.

Unguarded,
    my heart explodes,
    into a delightful convergence,
    a place without
    time
    or tasks.

Peace is pervasive.
I become indistinct,
    painted into the picture
    of all creation.
So that I might be yours
    alone.

This was also written on the pilgrimage to Italy in 2000. I think of it more as a poem of appreciation than a poem of love.

Abba, Father

Italy, 2000

Abba, Father
gentle wind,
undefiling.

Abba, Father,
mindful presence,
unremitting.

Abba, Father,
silent song,
everlasting.

Sometimes God puts someone in our isolated existences
to teach us how to make contact with other people.
Georgie Rodiger was that person for me.

Thank you Lord, for My Godmother

Thanksgiving, 1996

Lord,
your kindnesses to me and those I love
are too expansive to envision,
too exhaustive to remember.
Because of your graciousness,
I have become like the nested toy
of a Russian child,
each doll encapsulating another,
and another and another,
each more fragile, richer in detail,
complete,
each sufficient in and of itself,
though contained by another,
and containing another.

This, and you, complete me;
your vision of wholeness and holiness,

each of us contained and containing.
You have changed the horizon for me
and awakened my spirit to the richness
of the human mind and human heart
unified.

Gently, you have answered my unspoken,
unthought prayers for real connection,
given me the needed human islands
on which to stand and gather strength.
I am the liberated captive,
exploding with the freedom of emotional
movement,
excited and bewildered by the new world
you have given me.

How different from what I had first
envisioned,
that for which I prayed.
Those early pleas were for removals,
lessenings, anesthetizings.
You responded with an invitation for me
to embrace all that seemed damaged and
wait for the person carrying the anointing;
she would teach me.

And she came in Your fullness;
lovable and irascible,
bright and empowered,
devout and childlike,
charming and fragile.
Often I asked you, though already

knowing,
is this whom you have sent?

She mentored me
and tolerated me.
She laughed with me,
shared ideas with me.
We fought and forgave,
battled and grew stronger,
loyalty never an issue.
Here, you taught me, is where pain is
purposeful.
Here, you showed me, is how real
connection is forged.

Thank you.
I asked merely to survive
and you showered me with a life of
abundance.

My old name was melody-sought.
My new name is harmony-obtained.

Prophesy

Prophesy is God speaking through one of His children to the rest of those who are assembled. The "I" is God. Prophesy is usually spoken as it is given. Some groups require that it be written and screened before it can be shared. That's why I happen to have some written prophesy. It may have lost its timeliness and its intended audience. Maybe not. I am chagrinned to say that God is a better writer than I am.

ACT Temecula Retreat

July, 2004

You lift your hands to me
and offer your love;
I receive it.
I offer my love to you,
will you receive it?
Will you open yourselves to me?
Will you let me show you
how beloved you are?
Will you let me exchange my heart for your heart?
Will you let me be your God?

I love you above all else.
Will you love me above all else?
Will you surrender to me
and find the perfect freedom for which you
hunger?
Perfect freedom is perfect love
made manifest in you
by my perfection.

You weary yourselves needlessly
trying to follow me;
quiet your minds;
wait for my voice;
you will find yourselves where you need to be.

You cannot
stand firmly on your feet,
and call me your God;
only in defeat
am I fully yours;
fall on your knees
and let me teach you to stand.

Open your eyes;
I have lifted your blindness,
shown you my Kingdom,
signed you,
empowered you,
taken the world from you;
you are my beloved.

Why do you ask me
for that which you already have?
Your reticence
keeps you rooted in yourselves.

Prophesy - ACT Bay Area Retreat

September, 2002

Tragic,
how little is your faith;
tragic,
to lose your place;
tragic,
to hide your face;
tragic,
to deny my grace.
Surrender
even your tragedy.
I can bless it.
I can use it.

Give me your
   brokenness,
   willfulness,
   failures.

I will weave them
into the most beautiful
of all tapestries
to rest the eyes
    of the vigilant;
the terror
    of the indigent;
the souls
    of the hesitant.
I create with love;
I recreate with love.
I still
what you cannot.
I quicken
what you cannot.
For I alone am God,
your only solace.

I answer
    before you ask.
I care
    before you are ready.
I am
the invisible actual,
the unknowable given,
the eternal now.
You touch me too lightly,
claim too little.
Embrace me wholly;
I am who I am.

*L*ift your hands
as well as your eyes.
I will honor
your boldness.
Proclaim me
    shamelessly;
embrace me
    without reservation.
I have
no use
for only part of you.

Prophesy – Italy Pilgrimage

2000 – Year of Jubilation

The only perfect
place of balance
is the jurisdiction
of my heart.
The road in
is surrender.

You pray for love,
for life,
for ministry.
Pray first
for death.
I cannot plant
atop your chaos.

You must open your hand
to hold mine.
You must embrace your sorrow

to touch mine.
You must surrender your heart
To know mine.

*Y*our fear is a wall
without gates.
You cannot reach me
from where you are.

*W*orship
the wounds
I bore for you.
Don't worship
your own wounds.
They are bridges
to bring people to me,
blessings I have entrusted to you.
Seek me in them.

A field of flowers pleases my eye;
a flower alone brings a tear.

*T*he things you think I require,
    I don't.
The things you think I desire,
    I don't.
The things you think I admire,

I don't.
I choose to love you
because I am love
and you are my child.

Printed in the United States
79954LV00002B/1-150